40 Czech Recipes for Home

By: Kelly Johnson

Table of Contents

- Svíčková na Smetaně (Beef Sirloin with Cream Sauce)
- Bramboráky (Potato Pancakes)
- Kulajda (Creamy Potato Soup with Mushrooms)
- Vepřo-Knedlo-Zelo (Roast Pork with Dumplings and Sauerkraut)
- Švestkový Knedlík (Plum Dumplings)
- Smažený Sýr (Fried Cheese)
- Trdelník (Czech Cinnamon Pastry)
- Guláš (Czech Goulash)
- Houbový Kuba (Mushroom Barley)
- Zelňačka (Sauerkraut Soup)
- Ovocné Knedlíky (Fruit Dumplings)
- Palačinky (Czech Pancakes)
- Koprová Omáčka (Dill Sauce)
- Pečená Kachna (Roast Duck)
- Sýrové Noky (Czech Cheese Dumplings)
- Tvarohové Knedlíky (Quark Dumplings)
- Uzené (Smoked Meat)
- Fritule (Czech Doughnuts)
- Bramborový Salát (Potato Salad)
- Tatarský Biftek (Czech Tartare Steak)
- Smažený Kapr (Fried Carp)
- Zelňačka s Klobásou (Sauerkraut Soup with Sausage)
- Jablečný Závin (Apple Strudel)
- Kyselé Okurky (Czech Pickles)
- Vaječná Pomazánka (Egg Spread)
- Kyselo (Czech Sour Soup)
- Halušky s Brynzou (Dumplings with Bryndza Cheese)
- Česnečka (Garlic Soup)
- Liškové Pralinky (Hazelnut Pralines)
- Záviny (Czech Strudels)
- Polévka z Krupice (Semolina Soup)
- Klobásy (Czech Sausages)
- Perník (Czech Gingerbread)
- Pstruh na Paprice (Trout with Paprika Sauce)

- Třešňový Závin (Cherry Strudel)
- Kávový Koláč (Coffee Cake)
- Bílá Klobása (White Sausage)
- Kynuté Knedlíky (Yeast Dumplings)
- Bramboráčky (Potato Patties)
- Lívance (Czech Pancakes)

Svíčková na Smetaně (Beef Sirloin with Cream Sauce)

Ingredients:

For the beef:

- 800g beef sirloin
- 2 onions, chopped
- 2 carrots, chopped
- 2 celery stalks, chopped
- 2 bay leaves
- 6 black peppercorns
- 1 teaspoon salt
- 1 tablespoon vegetable oil

For the sauce:

- 2 cups beef broth
- 1 cup heavy cream
- 2 tablespoons unsalted butter
- 2 tablespoons all-purpose flour
- 2 tablespoons lemon juice
- 2 tablespoons sugar
- Salt and pepper to taste

For serving:

- 1 tablespoon cranberry sauce
- 1 tablespoon whipped cream
- 1 lemon, sliced
- 1 tablespoon chopped parsley

Instructions:

Preheat your oven to 180°C (350°F).

Season the beef sirloin with salt and pepper. In a large Dutch oven or oven-safe pot, heat vegetable oil over medium-high heat. Brown the beef on all sides until golden brown. Remove the beef from the pot and set aside.

In the same pot, add chopped onions, carrots, and celery. Sauté until softened, about 5-7 minutes.

Return the beef to the pot and add bay leaves and black peppercorns. Pour in beef broth until the beef is almost covered. Bring to a simmer.

Cover the pot and transfer it to the preheated oven. Cook for about 2-2.5 hours, or until the beef is tender and easily pierced with a fork.

Once the beef is cooked, remove it from the pot and set aside. Strain the cooking liquid, reserving the vegetables and discarding the bay leaves and peppercorns.

In a saucepan, melt butter over medium heat. Stir in flour to make a roux. Cook for 2 minutes, stirring constantly.

Gradually whisk in the reserved cooking liquid and heavy cream until smooth. Bring the sauce to a simmer, stirring frequently, until thickened.

Stir in lemon juice and sugar. Season with salt and pepper to taste.

Slice the beef thinly and serve it with the sauce. Garnish with cranberry sauce, whipped cream, lemon slices, and chopped parsley.

Enjoy your Svíčková na Smetaně with bread dumplings (knedlíky) or boiled potatoes for a traditional Czech meal!

Bramboráky (Potato Pancakes)

Ingredients:

- 4 large potatoes, peeled
- 1 small onion, finely chopped
- 2 eggs
- 3 tablespoons all-purpose flour
- 1 teaspoon baking powder
- 1 teaspoon salt
- 1/2 teaspoon black pepper
- Vegetable oil for frying
- Sour cream and chopped chives for serving (optional)

Instructions:

Grate the peeled potatoes using a box grater or a food processor. Place the grated potatoes in a clean kitchen towel or cheesecloth and squeeze out as much liquid as possible.
Transfer the grated potatoes to a large mixing bowl. Add the finely chopped onion, eggs, flour, baking powder, salt, and black pepper. Mix until well combined.
Heat a large skillet or frying pan over medium heat and add enough vegetable oil to cover the bottom of the pan.
Once the oil is hot, scoop about 1/4 cup of the potato mixture into the pan for each pancake. Flatten the mixture with a spatula to form pancakes about 1/4 inch thick.
Fry the pancakes for 3-4 minutes on each side, or until golden brown and crispy. You may need to adjust the heat to prevent burning.
Once cooked, transfer the pancakes to a plate lined with paper towels to drain any excess oil.
Repeat the process with the remaining potato mixture, adding more oil to the pan as needed.
Serve the bramboráky hot, topped with sour cream and chopped chives if desired.

Enjoy these delicious Czech potato pancakes as a side dish or a snack!

Kulajda (Creamy Potato Soup with Mushrooms)

Ingredients:

- 4 large potatoes, peeled and diced
- 1 onion, finely chopped
- 200g mushrooms, sliced
- 2 cloves garlic, minced
- 1 liter vegetable or chicken broth
- 250ml sour cream
- 2 tablespoons all-purpose flour
- 2 tablespoons butter
- 2 tablespoons vinegar
- 2 tablespoons chopped fresh dill
- Salt and pepper to taste
- Chopped fresh chives for garnish (optional)

Instructions:

In a large pot, melt the butter over medium heat. Add the chopped onion and garlic and sauté until softened, about 5 minutes.
Add the sliced mushrooms to the pot and cook until they release their moisture and start to brown, about 8-10 minutes.
Stir in the diced potatoes and cook for another 5 minutes, allowing them to slightly soften.
Sprinkle the flour over the vegetables and stir well to combine, cooking for another minute to cook out the raw flavor of the flour.
Slowly pour in the vegetable or chicken broth, stirring constantly to prevent lumps from forming. Bring the soup to a simmer and cook for about 15-20 minutes, or until the potatoes are tender.
In a small bowl, whisk together the sour cream and vinegar until smooth.
Gradually stir in a ladleful of hot soup to temper the sour cream mixture.
Pour the tempered sour cream mixture into the pot of soup, stirring well to combine. Allow the soup to simmer gently for another 5 minutes.
Stir in the chopped fresh dill and season the soup with salt and pepper to taste.
Ladle the kulajda into bowls and garnish with chopped fresh chives, if desired.
Serve hot and enjoy the comforting flavors of this creamy Czech potato soup with mushrooms!

Kulajda is often served with slices of hard-boiled egg on top for added richness and flavor. Feel free to customize it according to your preferences!

Vepřo-Knedlo-Zelo (Roast Pork with Dumplings and Sauerkraut)

Ingredients:

For the roast pork:

- 1.5 kg pork shoulder or pork loin
- 2 cloves garlic, minced
- 2 teaspoons caraway seeds
- 2 teaspoons salt
- 1 teaspoon black pepper
- 2 tablespoons vegetable oil

For the dumplings (knedlíky):

- 500g potatoes, peeled and grated
- 250g all-purpose flour
- 1 egg
- 1 teaspoon salt
- Water, as needed

For the sauerkraut (zelí):

- 500g sauerkraut
- 1 onion, finely chopped
- 2 tablespoons vegetable oil
- 1 tablespoon sugar
- Salt and pepper to taste

Instructions:

Preheat your oven to 180°C (350°F).
Prepare the roast pork: In a small bowl, mix together the minced garlic, caraway seeds, salt, and black pepper to make a paste. Rub the paste all over the pork shoulder or loin.
Heat vegetable oil in a large oven-safe skillet or roasting pan over medium-high heat. Sear the pork on all sides until golden brown, about 4-5 minutes per side.
Transfer the skillet or roasting pan to the preheated oven. Roast the pork for about 1.5 to 2 hours, or until the internal temperature reaches 70°C (160°F) and

the meat is tender. Cover the pork loosely with foil and let it rest for 10-15 minutes before slicing.

While the pork is roasting, prepare the dumplings: In a large mixing bowl, combine the grated potatoes, flour, egg, and salt. Mix well to form a dough. If the dough is too dry, add a little water as needed.

Divide the dough into equal portions and shape them into cylindrical dumplings. Bring a large pot of salted water to a boil. Carefully drop the dumplings into the boiling water and cook for about 15-20 minutes, or until they float to the surface and are cooked through.

Drain the dumplings and keep them warm.

Prepare the sauerkraut: In a large skillet, heat vegetable oil over medium heat. Add the chopped onion and sauté until softened, about 5 minutes.

Add the sauerkraut to the skillet along with the sugar, salt, and pepper. Cook, stirring occasionally, for about 10-15 minutes, or until the sauerkraut is heated through and tender.

Slice the roast pork and serve it with the dumplings and sauerkraut.

Enjoy your Vepřo-Knedlo-Zelo with a dollop of mustard or horseradish on the side for extra flavor!

This hearty Czech dish is perfect for a comforting meal on a cold day.

Švestkový Knedlík (Plum Dumplings)

Ingredients:

For the dough:

- 500g potatoes, boiled and mashed
- 200g all-purpose flour
- 1 egg
- Pinch of salt

For the filling:

- 12 ripe plums, pitted and halved
- 12 sugar cubes

For coating:

- 100g breadcrumbs
- 50g unsalted butter
- 2 tablespoons granulated sugar
- Ground cinnamon (optional)

Instructions:

Start by preparing the dough. In a large mixing bowl, combine the mashed potatoes, all-purpose flour, egg, and a pinch of salt. Knead the mixture until it forms a smooth dough. If the dough is too sticky, add a little more flour.
Divide the dough into 12 equal portions. Take each portion and flatten it into a small disc in the palm of your hand.
Place a halved plum in the center of each disc of dough. Add a sugar cube in the center of each plum half.
Carefully wrap the dough around the plum, shaping it into a smooth ball. Make sure the plum is completely enclosed by the dough.
Bring a large pot of salted water to a gentle boil.
Carefully drop the dumplings into the boiling water, making sure not to overcrowd the pot. Cook the dumplings in batches if necessary.

Let the dumplings cook for about 8-10 minutes, or until they float to the surface and are cooked through.

While the dumplings are cooking, prepare the breadcrumb coating. In a skillet, melt the unsalted butter over medium heat. Add the breadcrumbs and stir constantly until they turn golden brown and are toasted.

Once the dumplings are cooked, use a slotted spoon to remove them from the pot and drain any excess water.

Roll the cooked dumplings in the toasted breadcrumbs until they are evenly coated.

Arrange the plum dumplings on a serving platter or individual plates.

Sprinkle the dumplings with granulated sugar and ground cinnamon, if desired, for extra flavor.

Serve the švestkový knedlík warm as a delicious Czech dessert.

Enjoy these plum dumplings as a sweet treat that perfectly captures the flavors of late summer!

Smažený Sýr (Fried Cheese)

Ingredients:

- 200g cheese (typically Edam, Gouda, or another semi-hard cheese)
- 1 cup all-purpose flour
- 2 eggs
- 1 cup breadcrumbs
- Vegetable oil for frying
- Salt and pepper to taste
- Lemon wedges for serving

Instructions:

Begin by slicing the cheese into thick slices, about 1/2 inch in thickness. Pat the cheese slices dry with paper towels to remove any excess moisture.

Set up a breading station with three shallow dishes. Place the flour in the first dish, beat the eggs in the second dish, and pour the breadcrumbs into the third dish.

Season the flour with salt and pepper to taste.

Dredge each cheese slice in the flour, shaking off any excess. Dip it into the beaten eggs, ensuring it is fully coated. Finally, coat the cheese slice evenly with breadcrumbs, pressing gently to adhere.

Repeat the breading process for all the cheese slices and place them on a plate or baking sheet.

Heat vegetable oil in a large skillet or frying pan over medium-high heat. The oil should be hot enough to sizzle when you add the cheese slices.

Carefully place the breaded cheese slices in the hot oil, making sure not to overcrowd the pan. Fry the cheese slices for about 2-3 minutes on each side, or until they are golden brown and crispy.

Use a slotted spoon or spatula to transfer the fried cheese slices to a plate lined with paper towels to drain any excess oil.

Serve the smažený sýr hot, garnished with lemon wedges on the side.

Enjoy your crispy and delicious Czech Fried Cheese as a snack or a main course, accompanied by tartar sauce, ketchup, or your favorite dipping sauce!

This dish is often served with fries or a side salad for a complete meal. It's simple to make and incredibly satisfying to eat.

Trdelník (Czech Cinnamon Pastry)

Ingredients:

- 500g all-purpose flour
- 250ml warm milk
- 7g active dry yeast
- 50g granulated sugar
- 1/2 teaspoon salt
- 1 egg
- 100g unsalted butter, melted
- Vegetable oil, for greasing
- 100g granulated sugar
- 2 tablespoons ground cinnamon

Instructions:

In a small bowl, combine the warm milk and active dry yeast. Let it sit for about 5-10 minutes, or until the yeast is activated and foamy.

In a large mixing bowl, combine the flour, sugar, and salt. Make a well in the center and add the activated yeast mixture, beaten egg, and melted butter.

Mix the ingredients together to form a dough. Knead the dough on a lightly floured surface for about 5-7 minutes, or until it becomes smooth and elastic.

Place the dough in a greased bowl, cover it with a clean kitchen towel, and let it rise in a warm place for about 1-2 hours, or until it doubles in size.

Once the dough has risen, punch it down to release the air bubbles. Divide the dough into equal portions, depending on how many trdelníks you want to make. Roll each portion of dough into a long rope, about 1 inch in diameter.

Wrap the dough rope around a wooden or metal cylinder (traditionally, a wooden dowel or a special trdelník mold is used) in a spiral shape, making sure to overlap the layers slightly. Press the ends together to seal.

In a shallow dish, mix together the granulated sugar and ground cinnamon. Roll the shaped dough in the cinnamon-sugar mixture, ensuring it is evenly coated.

Preheat your oven to 180°C (350°F). Place the prepared trdelníks on a baking sheet lined with parchment paper.

Bake the trdelníks in the preheated oven for about 20-25 minutes, or until they are golden brown and cooked through.

Once baked, remove the trdelníks from the oven and let them cool slightly before serving.

Enjoy your freshly baked Czech cinnamon pastries as a delicious treat with a cup of coffee or tea!

Trdelníks are best enjoyed warm and fresh, but they can also be stored in an airtight container at room temperature for a day or two. Simply reheat them in the oven before serving, if desired.

Guláš (Czech Goulash)

Ingredients:

- 800g beef chuck, cut into bite-sized pieces
- 2 onions, finely chopped
- 2 cloves garlic, minced
- 2 tablespoons vegetable oil
- 2 tablespoons sweet paprika
- 1 teaspoon hot paprika (optional, for extra heat)
- 1 teaspoon caraway seeds
- 2 tablespoons tomato paste
- 2 cups beef broth
- 2 bay leaves
- Salt and pepper to taste
- Chopped fresh parsley for garnish (optional)
- Cooked egg noodles or bread dumplings for serving

Instructions:

Heat the vegetable oil in a large Dutch oven or heavy-bottomed pot over medium heat.
Add the chopped onions to the pot and sauté until they are soft and translucent, about 5-7 minutes.
Add the minced garlic to the pot and cook for another 1-2 minutes, until fragrant.
Increase the heat to medium-high and add the beef to the pot. Cook the beef, stirring occasionally, until it is browned on all sides.
Sprinkle the sweet paprika, hot paprika (if using), and caraway seeds over the beef and onions. Stir well to coat the meat evenly with the spices.
Stir in the tomato paste until it is well combined with the beef and onions.
Pour the beef broth into the pot and add the bay leaves. Bring the mixture to a simmer.
Reduce the heat to low, cover the pot, and let the goulash simmer gently for about 1.5 to 2 hours, or until the beef is tender and the flavors have melded together. Stir occasionally and add more broth if necessary to prevent the goulash from becoming too thick.
Once the beef is cooked through and tender, season the goulash with salt and pepper to taste.
Remove the bay leaves from the pot and discard them.

Serve the Czech goulash hot, garnished with chopped fresh parsley if desired, and accompanied by cooked egg noodles or bread dumplings.
Enjoy the rich and comforting flavors of this classic Czech dish!

Czech goulash is even better the next day, as the flavors continue to develop over time. Store any leftovers in the refrigerator and reheat gently on the stove before serving.

Houbový Kuba (Mushroom Barley)

Ingredients:

- 1 cup pearl barley
- 250g mushrooms (such as button mushrooms or cremini mushrooms), sliced
- 1 onion, finely chopped
- 2 cloves garlic, minced
- 2 tablespoons vegetable oil or butter
- 4 cups vegetable or mushroom broth
- 1 teaspoon dried marjoram
- 1/2 teaspoon dried thyme
- Salt and pepper to taste
- Chopped fresh parsley for garnish (optional)

Instructions:

Rinse the pearl barley under cold water until the water runs clear. Drain well and set aside.
In a large pot or Dutch oven, heat the vegetable oil or butter over medium heat.
Add the chopped onion to the pot and sauté until it becomes soft and translucent, about 5-7 minutes.
Add the minced garlic to the pot and cook for another 1-2 minutes, until fragrant.
Add the sliced mushrooms to the pot and cook until they release their moisture and start to brown, about 8-10 minutes.
Stir in the pearl barley and cook for another 2-3 minutes, stirring frequently.
Pour the vegetable or mushroom broth into the pot and bring the mixture to a simmer.
Add the dried marjoram and thyme to the pot, stirring well to combine.
Reduce the heat to low, cover the pot, and let the houbový kuba simmer gently for about 45-50 minutes, or until the barley is tender and cooked through. Stir occasionally and add more broth if necessary to achieve your desired consistency.
Once the barley is cooked, season the dish with salt and pepper to taste.
Serve the houbový kuba hot, garnished with chopped fresh parsley if desired.
Enjoy this comforting and nutritious Czech Mushroom Barley as a main course or a side dish!

This dish pairs well with crusty bread or a simple green salad for a complete meal. It's also great for meal prep, as it keeps well in the refrigerator for a few days and can be reheated easily.

Zelňačka (Sauerkraut Soup)

Ingredients:

- 500g sauerkraut, drained and rinsed
- 1 onion, finely chopped
- 2 cloves garlic, minced
- 2 potatoes, peeled and diced
- 2 carrots, peeled and diced
- 2 celery stalks, diced
- 1 bay leaf
- 1 teaspoon caraway seeds
- 1 liter vegetable or chicken broth
- 2 tablespoons vegetable oil
- Salt and pepper to taste
- Sour cream for serving (optional)
- Chopped fresh parsley for garnish (optional)

Instructions:

In a large pot, heat vegetable oil over medium heat. Add the chopped onion and sauté until it becomes soft and translucent, about 5-7 minutes.
Add the minced garlic to the pot and cook for another 1-2 minutes, until fragrant.
Stir in the diced potatoes, carrots, and celery to the pot. Cook for about 5 minutes, stirring occasionally.
Add the drained and rinsed sauerkraut to the pot, along with the bay leaf and caraway seeds. Cook for another 2-3 minutes, allowing the flavors to meld together.
Pour the vegetable or chicken broth into the pot, ensuring that all the vegetables are submerged. Bring the mixture to a simmer.
Reduce the heat to low, cover the pot, and let the zelňačka simmer gently for about 30-40 minutes, or until the vegetables are tender.
Once the soup is cooked through, season it with salt and pepper to taste.
Ladle the zelňačka into bowls and serve hot, garnished with a dollop of sour cream and chopped fresh parsley if desired.
Enjoy this comforting and flavorful Czech Sauerkraut Soup as a delicious starter or a light meal!

This soup is often served with crusty bread or traditional Czech bread dumplings (knedlíky). It's a great way to warm up on a cold day and enjoy the unique taste of sauerkraut in a hearty soup.

Ovocné Knedlíky (Fruit Dumplings)

Ingredients:

For the dough:

- 500g potatoes, peeled and boiled
- 200g all-purpose flour
- 1 egg
- Pinch of salt

For the filling:

- 12 small fruits of your choice (such as plums, apricots, strawberries, or cherries), pitted if necessary
- Sugar (optional, depending on the sweetness of the fruit)

For serving:

- Melted butter
- Ground cinnamon
- Powdered sugar
- Sour cream or whipped cream (optional)

Instructions:

Start by preparing the dough. In a large mixing bowl, mash the boiled potatoes until smooth.

Add the all-purpose flour, egg, and a pinch of salt to the mashed potatoes. Mix well to form a dough. If the dough is too sticky, add a little more flour.

Divide the dough into 12 equal portions.

Take each portion of dough and flatten it in the palm of your hand to form a small disc.

Place a small amount of sugar (if using) in the center of each dough disc, and then place a fruit in the center. If using larger fruits like peaches or apples, you may need to cut them into smaller pieces to fit inside the dough.

Carefully wrap the dough around the fruit, shaping it into a smooth ball. Make sure the fruit is completely enclosed by the dough.

Bring a large pot of salted water to a gentle boil.

Carefully drop the fruit-filled dumplings into the boiling water, making sure not to overcrowd the pot. Cook the dumplings in batches if necessary.

Let the dumplings cook for about 10-12 minutes, or until they float to the surface and are cooked through.

Use a slotted spoon to remove the cooked dumplings from the pot and drain any excess water.

Serve the ovocné knedlíky hot, drizzled with melted butter and sprinkled with ground cinnamon and powdered sugar.

Optionally, serve with sour cream or whipped cream on the side for dipping or dolloping.

Enjoy these delicious Czech Fruit Dumplings as a sweet treat or dessert!

These dumplings are best enjoyed warm and fresh, but they can also be stored in the refrigerator for a day or two and reheated gently before serving. Experiment with different fruits and flavorings to create your own unique variations!

Palačinky (Czech Pancakes)

Ingredients:

- 2 cups all-purpose flour
- 2 cups milk
- 2 eggs
- 2 tablespoons granulated sugar
- 1 teaspoon vanilla extract (optional)
- Pinch of salt
- Butter or oil for frying

Instructions:

In a large mixing bowl, whisk together the flour, milk, eggs, sugar, vanilla extract (if using), and a pinch of salt until smooth. The batter should be thin and pourable.

Heat a non-stick skillet or frying pan over medium heat. Add a small amount of butter or oil to the pan and swirl to coat the bottom evenly.

Pour a small ladleful of batter into the center of the pan and quickly tilt the pan in a circular motion to spread the batter thinly and evenly.

Cook the pancake for about 1-2 minutes, or until the edges start to lift and the bottom is golden brown.

Carefully flip the pancake using a spatula and cook for another 1-2 minutes on the other side, until golden brown.

Transfer the cooked pancake to a plate and cover with a clean kitchen towel to keep warm. Repeat the process with the remaining batter, adding more butter or oil to the pan as needed.

Serve the palačinky warm with your favorite toppings. Popular toppings include:
- Jam or fruit preserves
- Fresh fruit slices (such as strawberries, bananas, or blueberries)
- Nutella or chocolate spread
- Honey or maple syrup
- Whipped cream
- Powdered sugar
- Lemon juice

Roll or fold the palačinky with the desired toppings and enjoy them as a delicious breakfast or dessert!

These Czech pancakes are versatile and can be customized with various fillings and toppings to suit your preferences. Experiment with different flavors and enjoy this classic Czech treat!

Koprová Omáčka (Dill Sauce)

Ingredients:

- 2 tablespoons butter
- 2 tablespoons all-purpose flour
- 2 cups vegetable or chicken broth
- 1 cup sour cream
- 2 tablespoons chopped fresh dill
- 1 tablespoon lemon juice
- Salt and pepper to taste

Instructions:

In a saucepan, melt the butter over medium heat.
Stir in the all-purpose flour to make a roux. Cook the roux, stirring constantly, for about 1-2 minutes until it becomes golden brown and fragrant.
Gradually whisk in the vegetable or chicken broth, stirring constantly to prevent lumps from forming.
Bring the mixture to a simmer and cook for about 5 minutes, stirring occasionally, until the sauce thickens.
Reduce the heat to low and stir in the sour cream until well combined.
Add the chopped fresh dill and lemon juice to the sauce. Stir well to incorporate.
Season the sauce with salt and pepper to taste.
Continue to cook the sauce on low heat for another 2-3 minutes, stirring occasionally, until heated through.
Taste and adjust the seasoning if needed.
Remove the sauce from heat and serve it warm with boiled potatoes, boiled beef, or fish.
Garnish with additional chopped fresh dill if desired.
Enjoy the creamy and flavorful Czech Dill Sauce as a delicious accompaniment to your favorite dishes!

This sauce adds a refreshing and herbaceous flavor to your meal, making it a popular choice in Czech cuisine. Adjust the thickness of the sauce by adding more or less broth according to your preference.

Pečená Kachna (Roast Duck)

Ingredients:

- 1 whole duck (about 2-3 kg), cleaned and patted dry
- Salt and pepper to taste
- 1 onion, quartered
- 2 carrots, chopped into large chunks
- 2 celery stalks, chopped into large chunks
- 4 cloves garlic, smashed
- 2 sprigs fresh rosemary
- 2 sprigs fresh thyme
- 2 tablespoons vegetable oil or melted duck fat

For the gravy (optional):

- 2 tablespoons all-purpose flour
- 2 cups chicken or vegetable broth
- Salt and pepper to taste

Instructions:

Preheat your oven to 180°C (350°F).
Season the cleaned and dried duck generously with salt and pepper, both inside and outside the cavity.
Stuff the cavity of the duck with the quartered onion, chopped carrots, chopped celery, smashed garlic cloves, fresh rosemary, and fresh thyme.
Truss the duck by tying the legs together with kitchen twine and tucking the wings underneath the bird.
Place the duck on a rack in a roasting pan, breast side up.
Rub the skin of the duck with vegetable oil or melted duck fat to help it crisp up during roasting.
Roast the duck in the preheated oven for about 2.5 to 3 hours, or until the skin is golden brown and crispy, and the internal temperature of the thickest part of the thigh reaches 75°C (165°F). Baste the duck occasionally with the pan juices during roasting.
Once the duck is cooked through, remove it from the oven and let it rest for about 10-15 minutes before carving.

While the duck is resting, you can make the gravy. Pour off any excess fat from the roasting pan, leaving about 2 tablespoons of fat and juices. Place the roasting pan over medium heat on the stovetop.

Sprinkle the all-purpose flour into the pan drippings and whisk to combine, creating a roux. Cook the roux for about 1-2 minutes until it becomes golden brown.

Gradually whisk in the chicken or vegetable broth, scraping up any browned bits from the bottom of the pan. Bring the mixture to a simmer and cook for a few minutes until the gravy thickens.

Season the gravy with salt and pepper to taste.

Carve the roasted duck into serving portions and serve it with the gravy on the side.

Enjoy your delicious and flavorful Czech Roast Duck as a centerpiece for your festive meal!

Serve the roast duck with traditional Czech side dishes such as red cabbage, potato dumplings, or bread dumplings for a complete and satisfying meal.

Sýrové Noky (Czech Cheese Dumplings)

Ingredients:

- 500g potatoes, peeled and boiled
- 200g soft cheese (such as Tvaroh or farmer's cheese), drained
- 1 egg
- 100g all-purpose flour
- 50g breadcrumbs
- Salt and pepper to taste
- Butter or oil for frying

Instructions:

In a large mixing bowl, mash the boiled potatoes until smooth.

Add the soft cheese, egg, all-purpose flour, breadcrumbs, salt, and pepper to the bowl. Mix well until all the ingredients are fully combined and you have a dough-like consistency.

Bring a large pot of salted water to a boil.

With slightly wet hands, shape the dough into small dumplings, forming them into oval shapes or balls. You can adjust the size according to your preference.

Carefully drop the dumplings into the boiling water, working in batches if necessary to avoid overcrowding the pot. Cook the dumplings for about 5-7 minutes, or until they float to the surface and are cooked through.

While the dumplings are cooking, prepare a skillet or frying pan over medium heat. Add butter or oil to the pan.

Using a slotted spoon, transfer the cooked dumplings to the skillet. Fry the dumplings for about 2-3 minutes on each side, or until they are golden brown and crispy.

Once the dumplings are golden brown on both sides, remove them from the skillet and place them on a plate lined with paper towels to drain any excess oil.

Serve the sýrové noky hot as a main course or side dish, garnished with chopped fresh herbs or a dollop of sour cream if desired.

Enjoy the delicious and cheesy Czech Cheese Dumplings as a comforting and satisfying dish!

These dumplings can be served on their own or accompanied by a salad or vegetable side dish for a complete meal. They're a great way to enjoy the rich flavors of cheese in a hearty and comforting dish.

Tvarohové Knedlíky (Quark Dumplings)

Ingredients:

For the dough:

- 500g quark (Tvaroh or farmer's cheese)
- 1 egg
- 1 tablespoon granulated sugar
- Pinch of salt
- About 200g all-purpose flour (plus extra for dusting)

For the filling (optional):

- Fruit jam or preserves (such as plum, apricot, or strawberry)

For serving:

- Melted butter
- Powdered sugar
- Ground cinnamon

Instructions:

In a large mixing bowl, combine the quark, egg, granulated sugar, and a pinch of salt. Mix well until smooth.

Gradually add the all-purpose flour to the quark mixture, stirring continuously, until you have a soft and slightly sticky dough. The amount of flour needed may vary depending on the consistency of the quark.

Turn the dough out onto a floured surface and knead it gently for a few minutes until it becomes smooth and pliable.

Divide the dough into equal portions and flatten each portion into a small disc in the palm of your hand.

If desired, place a small amount of fruit jam or preserves in the center of each dough disc. Fold the dough over the filling, shaping it into a smooth ball. Make sure the filling is completely enclosed by the dough.

Bring a large pot of salted water to a gentle boil.

Carefully drop the filled dumplings into the boiling water, working in batches if necessary to avoid overcrowding the pot. Cook the dumplings for about 10-12 minutes, or until they float to the surface and are cooked through.

While the dumplings are cooking, prepare a skillet or frying pan over medium heat. Add melted butter to the pan.

Once the dumplings are cooked, use a slotted spoon to transfer them to the skillet. Fry the dumplings for about 2-3 minutes on each side, or until they are golden brown and crispy.

Remove the fried dumplings from the skillet and place them on a plate lined with paper towels to drain any excess oil.

Serve the tvarohové knedlíky hot, sprinkled with powdered sugar and ground cinnamon if desired.

Enjoy these delicious and indulgent Czech Quark Dumplings as a sweet dessert or a special treat!

These dumplings are best enjoyed warm and fresh, but they can also be stored in the refrigerator for a day or two and reheated gently before serving. Adjust the sweetness according to your preference and experiment with different fruit fillings for variety!

Uzené (Smoked Meat)

Ingredients:

- Meat of your choice (commonly pork, beef, or poultry)
- Salt
- Spices (optional, such as black pepper, garlic powder, paprika)
- Wood chips or chunks for smoking (traditionally beechwood or fruitwoods are used)

Instructions:

Choose the type of meat you'd like to smoke. Pork is a popular choice, especially cuts like pork shoulder or pork ribs, but you can also use beef, poultry, or game meats.

Trim any excess fat from the meat and pat it dry with paper towels.

Season the meat generously with salt. You can also add other spices or seasonings according to your preference, such as black pepper, garlic powder, or paprika.

Prepare your smoker according to the manufacturer's instructions. If you're using a charcoal smoker, light the charcoal and wait until it's ashed over before adding the wood chips or chunks for smoking. If you're using an electric smoker, simply add the wood chips or chunks to the designated tray.

Once the smoker is at the desired temperature (typically around 225-250°F or 107-121°C), place the seasoned meat on the grates.

Close the lid of the smoker and let the meat smoke for several hours, depending on the type and size of the meat. Pork shoulder, for example, may take 6-8 hours or more to fully cook and become tender.

Monitor the temperature of the smoker and the internal temperature of the meat using a meat thermometer. The meat is done when it reaches an internal temperature of at least 145°F (63°C) for pork and beef, or 165°F (74°C) for poultry.

Once the meat is done smoking, remove it from the smoker and let it rest for a few minutes before slicing and serving.

Serve the uzené as a main course with side dishes like sauerkraut, potato salad, or bread dumplings. Alternatively, you can use it as an ingredient in soups, stews, or sandwiches.

Enjoy the rich, smoky flavor of this traditional Czech smoked meat dish!

Remember to always follow proper food safety guidelines when smoking meat, including ensuring that the meat reaches a safe internal temperature to prevent foodborne illness.

Fritule (Czech Doughnuts)

Ingredients:

- 2 cups all-purpose flour
- 2 eggs
- 1 cup milk
- 1/4 cup granulated sugar
- 1 tablespoon rum (optional)
- Zest of 1 lemon
- 1 teaspoon baking powder
- 1/4 teaspoon salt
- Vegetable oil for frying
- Powdered sugar for dusting

Instructions:

In a mixing bowl, whisk together the eggs, sugar, milk, and rum (if using) until well combined.

Add the lemon zest to the egg mixture and mix again.

In a separate bowl, sift together the flour, baking powder, and salt.

Gradually add the dry ingredients to the wet ingredients, stirring until a smooth batter forms. The batter should be thick but still pourable. If it's too thick, you can add a little more milk.

If desired, fold in a handful of raisins into the batter.

Heat vegetable oil in a deep fryer or large, deep skillet to 350°F (175°C).

Using a small spoon or cookie scoop, carefully drop small portions of the batter into the hot oil, working in batches to avoid overcrowding the fryer.

Fry the fritule for about 2-3 minutes on each side, or until they are golden brown and cooked through. Use a slotted spoon to remove them from the oil and transfer them to a plate lined with paper towels to drain any excess oil.

Once all the fritule are fried, dust them generously with powdered sugar while they are still warm.

Serve the fritule warm as a delicious snack or dessert, and enjoy their fluffy texture and delicate flavor!

These Czech doughnuts are best enjoyed fresh and warm, but they can also be stored in an airtight container at room temperature for a day or two. Reheat them briefly in the oven before serving if they lose their crispiness.

Bramborový Salát (Potato Salad)

Ingredients:

- 1 kg potatoes (preferably waxy potatoes such as Yukon Gold or red potatoes)
- 3-4 hard-boiled eggs, chopped
- 1 onion, finely chopped
- 1-2 pickles (gherkins), finely chopped
- 200g mayonnaise
- 2 tablespoons mustard
- 2 tablespoons white vinegar or pickle juice (from the gherkins)
- Salt and pepper to taste
- Chopped fresh dill or parsley for garnish (optional)

Instructions:

Wash and scrub the potatoes, then place them in a large pot of salted water. Bring the water to a boil and cook the potatoes until they are tender when pierced with a fork, about 15-20 minutes depending on their size.

Drain the potatoes and let them cool slightly. Once cool enough to handle, peel the potatoes and cut them into bite-sized cubes.

In a large mixing bowl, combine the chopped potatoes, hard-boiled eggs, finely chopped onion, and chopped pickles.

In a separate small bowl, whisk together the mayonnaise, mustard, and white vinegar or pickle juice to make the dressing. Season with salt and pepper to taste.

Pour the dressing over the potato mixture and gently toss until all the ingredients are evenly coated.

Taste the potato salad and adjust the seasoning if necessary, adding more salt, pepper, mustard, or vinegar according to your preference.

Cover the potato salad and refrigerate it for at least 1 hour before serving to allow the flavors to meld together.

Before serving, garnish the potato salad with chopped fresh dill or parsley if desired.

Serve the bramborový salát cold as a side dish with grilled meats, sausages, or as part of a festive meal.

Enjoy the creamy and flavorful Czech Potato Salad as a delicious accompaniment to your favorite dishes!

Feel free to customize the potato salad according to your taste preferences by adding ingredients like chopped celery, bacon, green onions, or grated carrots.

Tatarský Biftek (Czech Tartare Steak)

Ingredients:

- 400g beef tenderloin or top sirloin, very finely chopped
- 1 small onion, finely chopped
- 2 tablespoons capers, finely chopped
- 2 tablespoons gherkins (pickles), finely chopped
- 2 tablespoons fresh parsley, finely chopped
- 1 tablespoon Dijon mustard
- 1 tablespoon Worcestershire sauce
- 1 tablespoon ketchup
- 1 tablespoon olive oil
- 1 tablespoon lemon juice
- Salt and pepper to taste
- Tabasco sauce or hot sauce (optional, for extra heat)
- Toasted bread or baguette slices, for serving
- Mixed greens or lettuce leaves, for garnish (optional)

Instructions:

Start by ensuring your beef is very finely chopped. You can use a sharp knife to finely dice the beef, or you can ask your butcher to do it for you.

In a large mixing bowl, combine the finely chopped beef with the chopped onion, capers, gherkins, and fresh parsley.

In a small bowl, whisk together the Dijon mustard, Worcestershire sauce, ketchup, olive oil, and lemon juice until well combined.

Pour the dressing over the beef mixture and toss until everything is evenly coated.

Season the tartare steak mixture with salt and pepper to taste. If you like it spicy, you can also add a few dashes of Tabasco sauce or your favorite hot sauce.

Cover the bowl with plastic wrap and refrigerate the tartare steak mixture for at least 30 minutes to allow the flavors to meld together.

Before serving, taste the tartare steak mixture and adjust the seasoning if necessary.

To serve, shape the tartare steak mixture into small mounds or quenelles using a spoon. Alternatively, you can use a ring mold to create neat portions.

Arrange the tartare steak portions on serving plates alongside toasted bread or baguette slices.
Garnish the plates with mixed greens or lettuce leaves if desired.
Serve the tatarský biftek immediately as a sophisticated appetizer, allowing guests to spread the tartare steak on the toasted bread or baguette slices.
Enjoy the bold and savory flavors of this Czech Tartare Steak as a delicious starter or light meal!

Remember to use the freshest and highest quality beef for tartare steak, as it's served raw. Additionally, handle raw meat with care and follow food safety guidelines to minimize the risk of foodborne illness.

Smažený Kapr (Fried Carp)

Ingredients:

- 1 whole carp, cleaned and scaled (about 1-1.5 kg)
- Salt and pepper to taste
- All-purpose flour for dredging
- Vegetable oil or lard for frying
- Lemon wedges for serving
- Chopped fresh parsley for garnish (optional)

Instructions:

Rinse the cleaned and scaled carp under cold water and pat it dry with paper towels. Make sure to remove any excess moisture from the fish.

Season the carp generously with salt and pepper, both inside and outside the cavity.

Heat vegetable oil or lard in a large skillet or frying pan over medium-high heat. You'll need enough oil to submerge the carp halfway.

While the oil is heating, dredge the seasoned carp in all-purpose flour, shaking off any excess.

Carefully place the carp in the hot oil, laying it away from you to prevent any splattering. Fry the carp for about 5-7 minutes on each side, or until it is golden brown and crispy.

Use a spatula or fish turner to carefully flip the carp halfway through cooking to ensure even browning.

Once the carp is cooked through and golden brown on both sides, carefully remove it from the oil and transfer it to a plate lined with paper towels to drain any excess oil.

Let the fried carp rest for a few minutes before serving to allow the juices to redistribute.

Serve the smažený kapr hot, garnished with chopped fresh parsley if desired and accompanied by lemon wedges for squeezing over the fish.

Enjoy the crispy and flavorful Czech Fried Carp as a delicious and traditional holiday dish!

Smažený kapr is often served with potato salad, sauerkraut, or other traditional Czech side dishes. It's a festive and hearty meal that's sure to be enjoyed by family and friends during the holiday season.

Zelňačka s Klobásou (Sauerkraut Soup with Sausage)

Ingredients:

- 500g sauerkraut, drained and rinsed
- 300g smoked sausage or kielbasa, sliced
- 1 onion, chopped
- 2 cloves garlic, minced
- 2 potatoes, peeled and diced
- 2 carrots, peeled and diced
- 2 celery stalks, diced
- 1 bay leaf
- 1 teaspoon caraway seeds
- 1 liter vegetable or chicken broth
- 2 tablespoons vegetable oil or butter
- Salt and pepper to taste
- Chopped fresh parsley for garnish (optional)

Instructions:

In a large pot or Dutch oven, heat the vegetable oil or butter over medium heat. Add the chopped onion to the pot and sauté until it becomes soft and translucent, about 5-7 minutes.
Add the minced garlic to the pot and cook for another 1-2 minutes, until fragrant.
Add the sliced smoked sausage or kielbasa to the pot and cook until it starts to brown, about 5 minutes.
Stir in the diced potatoes, carrots, and celery to the pot. Cook for another 5 minutes, stirring occasionally.
Add the drained and rinsed sauerkraut to the pot, along with the bay leaf and caraway seeds. Cook for another 2-3 minutes, allowing the flavors to meld together.
Pour the vegetable or chicken broth into the pot, ensuring that all the vegetables and sausage are submerged. Bring the mixture to a simmer.
Reduce the heat to low, cover the pot, and let the zelňačka simmer gently for about 30-40 minutes, or until the vegetables are tender.
Once the soup is cooked through, season it with salt and pepper to taste.
Serve the zelňačka hot, garnished with chopped fresh parsley if desired.

Enjoy this comforting and hearty Czech Sauerkraut Soup with Sausage as a delicious main course or starter!

This soup pairs well with crusty bread or traditional Czech bread dumplings (knedlíky). It's a great way to warm up on a cold day and enjoy the unique flavors of sauerkraut and smoked sausage.

Jablečný Závin (Apple Strudel)

Ingredients:

For the dough:

- 2 cups all-purpose flour
- 1/4 teaspoon salt
- 2 tablespoons vegetable oil
- 3/4 cup lukewarm water
- 1 tablespoon white vinegar

For the filling:

- 4-5 large apples (such as Granny Smith), peeled, cored, and thinly sliced
- 1/2 cup granulated sugar
- 1 teaspoon ground cinnamon
- 1/2 cup raisins (optional)
- 1/2 cup breadcrumbs
- 1/2 cup melted butter, divided

For brushing:

- 2 tablespoons melted butter
- Powdered sugar for dusting

Instructions:

Preheat your oven to 180°C (350°F) and line a baking sheet with parchment paper.

In a large mixing bowl, combine the flour and salt. Make a well in the center and add the vegetable oil, lukewarm water, and white vinegar. Mix until a smooth dough forms. If the dough is too sticky, add a little more flour.

Knead the dough on a floured surface for about 5-7 minutes, or until it becomes smooth and elastic. Form the dough into a ball, cover it with a clean kitchen towel, and let it rest for about 30 minutes.

While the dough is resting, prepare the filling. In a separate bowl, toss together the thinly sliced apples, granulated sugar, ground cinnamon, and raisins (if using).

Roll out the dough on a floured surface into a thin rectangle, about 12x16 inches in size.

Sprinkle the breadcrumbs evenly over the rolled-out dough, leaving about an inch border around the edges.

Arrange the apple filling evenly over the breadcrumbs.

Drizzle half of the melted butter over the apple filling.

Starting from one long side, carefully roll up the dough jelly-roll style, enclosing the filling.

Transfer the rolled strudel onto the prepared baking sheet, seam side down.

Brush the top of the strudel with the remaining melted butter.

Using a sharp knife, make several diagonal slashes on the top of the strudel to allow steam to escape during baking.

Bake the apple strudel in the preheated oven for about 35-40 minutes, or until it is golden brown and crispy.

Remove the strudel from the oven and let it cool slightly on the baking sheet.

Once cooled, dust the apple strudel with powdered sugar.

Slice the strudel into pieces and serve warm or at room temperature.

Enjoy the delicious Czech Jablečný Závin (Apple Strudel) as a delightful dessert or sweet treat!

This apple strudel is best enjoyed fresh on the day it's baked, but leftovers can be stored in an airtight container at room temperature for a day or two.

Kyselé Okurky (Czech Pickles)

Ingredients:

- 1 kg small cucumbers (kirby or gherkin variety work well)
- 1 liter water
- 250 ml vinegar (white or apple cider vinegar)
- 80g salt
- 2-3 cloves garlic, peeled and crushed
- 1-2 bay leaves
- 1-2 teaspoons whole black peppercorns
- 1-2 teaspoons whole mustard seeds
- Fresh dill (optional)

Instructions:

Rinse the cucumbers thoroughly under cold water to remove any dirt or debris. Trim off both ends of each cucumber and prick them with a fork or small knife.
In a large pot, combine the water, vinegar, and salt. Bring the mixture to a boil, stirring until the salt has dissolved completely.
Remove the pot from the heat and let the brine cool to room temperature.
In clean, sterilized jars, place the crushed garlic cloves, bay leaves, black peppercorns, mustard seeds, and fresh dill (if using).
Pack the cucumbers tightly into the jars, leaving a little space at the top.
Pour the cooled brine over the cucumbers, ensuring they are completely submerged. You may need to weigh them down with a small plate or jar lid to keep them submerged.
Seal the jars tightly with lids and store them in a cool, dark place for at least 1-2 weeks to allow the flavors to develop.
Once opened, store the pickles in the refrigerator and consume them within a few weeks.
Enjoy your homemade kyselé okurky as a tasty snack or as an accompaniment to your favorite Czech dishes!

Feel free to adjust the seasoning and spices according to your taste preferences. You can also experiment with adding other ingredients like sliced onions, chili peppers, or fresh herbs to customize your pickles. Homemade Czech pickles are a delicious and versatile addition to any pantry.

Vaječná Pomazánka (Egg Spread)

Ingredients:

- 4 hard-boiled eggs
- 2-3 tablespoons mayonnaise
- 1 teaspoon mustard
- 1 tablespoon chopped fresh chives or parsley (optional)
- Salt and pepper to taste
- Paprika for garnish (optional)

Instructions:

Peel the hard-boiled eggs and chop them finely using a knife or egg slicer.
In a mixing bowl, combine the chopped eggs with mayonnaise and mustard. Start with 2 tablespoons of mayonnaise and add more if needed to reach your desired consistency.
Add chopped fresh chives or parsley to the mixture for extra flavor, if desired.
Season the egg spread with salt and pepper to taste. Mix well to combine all the ingredients evenly.
Taste the spread and adjust the seasoning or mayonnaise according to your preference.
Transfer the vaječná pomazánka to a serving bowl and sprinkle with paprika for garnish, if desired.
Serve the egg spread on bread, toast, or crackers as a delicious snack or appetizer.
Enjoy the creamy and flavorful Czech Egg Spread as a versatile addition to your meals!

Feel free to customize the egg spread by adding other ingredients such as chopped pickles, onions, or fresh herbs. You can also adjust the consistency by adding more or less mayonnaise. Experiment with different variations to suit your taste preferences!

Kyselo (Czech Sour Soup)

Ingredients:

- 200g dried mushrooms (such as porcini or wild mushrooms)
- 1 onion, finely chopped
- 2 cloves garlic, minced
- 2 tablespoons vegetable oil or butter
- 1 liter vegetable or mushroom broth
- 2-3 tablespoons vinegar (white or apple cider vinegar)
- 2-3 tablespoons granulated sugar
- 250g sour cream
- 2 eggs
- Salt and pepper to taste
- Chopped fresh parsley for garnish (optional)

Instructions:

Start by soaking the dried mushrooms in hot water for about 30 minutes, or until they become soft. Once softened, drain the mushrooms, reserving the soaking liquid, and chop them into bite-sized pieces.

In a large pot, heat the vegetable oil or butter over medium heat. Add the chopped onion and minced garlic, and sauté until they become soft and translucent, about 5 minutes.

Add the chopped mushrooms to the pot and cook for another 5 minutes, stirring occasionally.

Pour the vegetable or mushroom broth into the pot, along with the reserved soaking liquid from the mushrooms. Bring the mixture to a simmer and cook for about 15-20 minutes, allowing the flavors to meld together.

In a small bowl, whisk together the sour cream and eggs until smooth.

Slowly pour a ladleful of the hot soup into the sour cream mixture, whisking constantly to temper the eggs and prevent them from curdling.

Gradually add the tempered sour cream mixture back into the pot of soup, stirring constantly to combine.

Season the soup with vinegar, sugar, salt, and pepper to taste. Adjust the seasoning according to your preference, adding more vinegar for extra sourness or sugar to balance the acidity.

Continue to simmer the soup for another 5-10 minutes, stirring occasionally, until it thickens slightly.

Once the soup is ready, remove it from the heat and let it cool slightly before serving.
Garnish the kyselo with chopped fresh parsley, if desired, and serve it hot as a comforting and flavorful Czech Sour Soup!

Enjoy this hearty and tangy soup as a delicious appetizer or light meal, accompanied by crusty bread or traditional Czech dumplings.

Halušky s Brynzou (Dumplings with Bryndza Cheese)

Ingredients:

For the halušky (dumplings):

- 500g potatoes, peeled and grated
- 250g all-purpose flour
- 1 egg
- Salt to taste

For the bryndza sauce:

- 250g bryndza cheese (or substitute with feta cheese mixed with sour cream)
- 2 tablespoons butter
- Optional toppings: cooked and crumbled bacon, fried onions, chopped chives or parsley

Instructions:

Start by preparing the halušky (dumplings). In a large mixing bowl, combine the grated potatoes, flour, egg, and salt. Mix until a dough forms.
Bring a large pot of salted water to a boil.
Using a spoon or a special halušky maker (if available), drop small portions of the dough into the boiling water. Cook the dumplings until they rise to the surface, then cook for an additional 2-3 minutes.
Use a slotted spoon to transfer the cooked dumplings to a colander to drain.
While the dumplings are cooking, prepare the bryndza sauce. In a small saucepan, melt the butter over low heat. Add the bryndza cheese and stir until it melts and forms a smooth sauce. If the sauce is too thick, you can thin it out with a little milk or cream.
Once the dumplings are cooked and drained, transfer them to a serving dish.
Pour the bryndza sauce over the dumplings, making sure to coat them evenly.
If desired, sprinkle cooked and crumbled bacon, fried onions, or chopped chives or parsley over the top for extra flavor and texture.
Serve the halušky s brynzou hot as a delicious and comforting dish, accompanied by a green salad or pickles on the side.

Enjoy this traditional Slovak and Czech delicacy with its unique combination of flavors and textures!

Česnečka (Garlic Soup)

Ingredients:

- 6 cups chicken or vegetable broth
- 6 cloves garlic, minced
- 2 large potatoes, peeled and diced
- 2 slices of bread, cubed
- 2 eggs
- 2 tablespoons olive oil or butter
- 1 teaspoon dried marjoram
- Salt and pepper to taste
- Chopped fresh parsley for garnish
- Optional: grated cheese for topping

Instructions:

In a large pot, heat the olive oil or butter over medium heat. Add the minced garlic and sauté for 1-2 minutes until fragrant, but be careful not to burn it.

Pour the chicken or vegetable broth into the pot and bring it to a simmer.

Add the diced potatoes and dried marjoram to the pot. Cook for about 15-20 minutes, or until the potatoes are tender.

While the soup is simmering, toast the bread cubes in a separate skillet until golden brown and crispy.

In a small bowl, whisk the eggs together until well beaten.

Once the potatoes are tender, slowly pour the beaten eggs into the simmering soup while stirring continuously. The eggs will cook and form ribbons in the soup.

Season the soup with salt and pepper to taste, adjusting the seasoning as needed.

To serve, ladle the hot česnečka into bowls. Garnish each bowl with toasted bread cubes and chopped fresh parsley.

Optionally, sprinkle grated cheese on top of each serving for extra flavor.

Serve the garlic soup hot as a comforting and flavorful dish, perfect for cold winter days or whenever you're craving a hearty soup!

Enjoy the robust garlic flavor and comforting warmth of this traditional Czech Česnečka!

Liškové Pralinky (Hazelnut Pralines)

Ingredients:

- 1 cup hazelnuts
- 1 cup granulated sugar
- 1/4 cup water
- 1 tablespoon unsalted butter
- 1/2 teaspoon vanilla extract
- Pinch of salt

Instructions:

Preheat your oven to 350°F (175°C). Spread the hazelnuts evenly on a baking sheet and toast them in the preheated oven for about 10-15 minutes, or until they are lightly browned and fragrant. Keep an eye on them to prevent burning.

Once toasted, remove the hazelnuts from the oven and let them cool slightly. Rub them between your hands or in a kitchen towel to remove as much of the skins as possible.

In a heavy-bottomed saucepan, combine the granulated sugar and water over medium heat. Stir until the sugar is dissolved.

Increase the heat to medium-high and bring the mixture to a boil. Cook, without stirring, until the sugar syrup reaches a light amber color, swirling the pan occasionally to ensure even cooking.

Once the syrup has reached the desired color, remove the saucepan from the heat. Carefully stir in the toasted hazelnuts, butter, vanilla extract, and a pinch of salt. The mixture will bubble up, so be cautious.

Quickly pour the hazelnut mixture onto a parchment-lined baking sheet, spreading it out into an even layer with a spatula.

Let the praline mixture cool and harden at room temperature for about 30 minutes to 1 hour.

Once hardened, break the praline into pieces or cut it into squares using a sharp knife.

Store the hazelnut pralines in an airtight container at room temperature for up to 1 week, or in the refrigerator for longer shelf life.

Enjoy these delicious Liškové pralinky as a sweet indulgence or package them up as homemade gifts for friends and family!

These homemade hazelnut pralines are sure to impress with their crunchy texture and rich, nutty flavor. Feel free to customize them by adding a sprinkle of sea salt on top or dipping them in melted chocolate for an extra special touch.

Záviny (Czech Strudels)

Ingredients for the dough:

- 2 cups all-purpose flour
- 1/4 teaspoon salt
- 1/4 cup vegetable oil
- 3/4 cup lukewarm water
- 1 tablespoon white vinegar

Ingredients for the apple filling:

- 4-5 medium-sized apples, peeled, cored, and thinly sliced
- 1/2 cup granulated sugar
- 1 teaspoon ground cinnamon
- 1/4 cup raisins (optional)
- 1/4 cup breadcrumbs
- 2 tablespoons unsalted butter, melted

Instructions:

Preheat your oven to 375°F (190°C) and line a baking sheet with parchment paper.

In a large mixing bowl, combine the flour and salt. Make a well in the center and add the vegetable oil, lukewarm water, and white vinegar. Mix until a smooth dough forms. If the dough is too sticky, add a little more flour.

Knead the dough on a floured surface for about 5-7 minutes, or until it becomes smooth and elastic. Form the dough into a ball, cover it with a clean kitchen towel, and let it rest for about 30 minutes.

While the dough is resting, prepare the apple filling. In a mixing bowl, combine the thinly sliced apples, granulated sugar, ground cinnamon, and raisins (if using). Toss until the apples are evenly coated.

Roll out the dough on a floured surface into a large rectangle, about 1/8 inch thick.

Sprinkle the breadcrumbs evenly over the rolled-out dough, leaving a border around the edges.

Arrange the apple filling evenly over the breadcrumbs.

Drizzle the melted butter over the apple filling.

Starting from one long side, carefully roll up the dough jelly-roll style, enclosing the filling.

Transfer the rolled strudel onto the prepared baking sheet, seam side down.

Brush the top of the strudel with a little extra melted butter for a golden finish.

Bake the strudel in the preheated oven for about 30-35 minutes, or until it is golden brown and crispy.

Remove the strudel from the oven and let it cool slightly on the baking sheet.

Once cooled, slice the strudel into pieces and serve warm or at room temperature.

Enjoy the delicious Czech záviny filled with sweet apple filling as a delightful dessert or sweet treat!

Feel free to customize the filling by using other fruits like cherries or apricots, or experiment with savory fillings like cabbage and mushrooms for a different flavor profile.

Polévka z Krupice (Semolina Soup)

Ingredients:

- 1/2 cup semolina (krupice)
- 4 cups chicken or vegetable broth
- 1 carrot, peeled and diced
- 1 celery stalk, diced
- 1 small onion, finely chopped
- 2 cloves garlic, minced
- 2 tablespoons butter or vegetable oil
- Salt and pepper to taste
- Chopped fresh parsley for garnish (optional)

Instructions:

In a large pot, heat the butter or vegetable oil over medium heat. Add the chopped onion and minced garlic, and sauté until they become soft and translucent, about 5 minutes.
Add the diced carrot and celery to the pot, and cook for another 3-4 minutes, stirring occasionally.
Pour the chicken or vegetable broth into the pot and bring it to a boil.
Gradually sprinkle the semolina into the boiling broth while stirring continuously to prevent lumps from forming.
Reduce the heat to low and let the soup simmer for about 10-15 minutes, or until the vegetables are tender and the semolina is cooked through. Stir occasionally to prevent sticking.
Once the soup has thickened to your desired consistency and the semolina is fully cooked, season it with salt and pepper to taste. Adjust the seasoning as needed.
Remove the soup from the heat and let it cool slightly before serving.
Ladle the warm polévka z krupice into serving bowls and garnish with chopped fresh parsley, if desired.
Serve the semolina soup hot as a comforting and nourishing dish, accompanied by crusty bread or crackers on the side.

Enjoy the creamy texture and hearty flavor of this traditional Czech Semolina Soup as a satisfying meal for lunch or dinner!

Klobásy (Czech Sausages)

Ingredients:

- 1 kg ground pork (you can also use a mixture of pork and beef)
- 2-3 cloves garlic, minced
- 1 tablespoon sweet paprika
- 1 teaspoon ground black pepper
- 1 teaspoon ground cumin
- 1 teaspoon ground coriander
- 1 teaspoon mustard seeds (optional)
- 1 teaspoon salt, or to taste
- Hog casings (natural sausage casings)

Instructions:

Rinse the hog casings under cold water to remove any salt and debris. Soak them in lukewarm water for at least 30 minutes to soften.

In a large mixing bowl, combine the ground pork with minced garlic, sweet paprika, ground black pepper, ground cumin, ground coriander, mustard seeds (if using), and salt. Mix well until all the spices are evenly distributed throughout the meat.

Prepare your sausage stuffer according to the manufacturer's instructions, and thread the softened hog casings onto the nozzle.

Stuff the seasoned meat mixture into the hog casings, ensuring that the sausages are evenly filled but not overstuffed to avoid bursting during cooking. Twist the sausages into links of your desired length.

Once all the sausages are stuffed, you can either grill them, smoke them, or boil them depending on your preference:

- Grilling: Preheat your grill to medium-high heat. Grill the sausages for about 5-7 minutes per side, or until they are cooked through and have a golden brown exterior.
- Smoking: Prepare your smoker according to the manufacturer's instructions. Smoke the sausages at a low temperature (around 225°F or 107°C) for about 1-2 hours, or until they reach an internal temperature of 160°F (71°C).
- Boiling: Bring a large pot of water to a boil. Add the sausages and reduce the heat to low. Simmer the sausages for about 20-30 minutes, or until they are cooked through.

Once the sausages are cooked, remove them from the grill, smoker, or pot, and let them rest for a few minutes before serving.
Serve the klobásy hot with your favorite condiments, such as mustard, horseradish, or sauerkraut.

Enjoy these homemade Czech sausages as a delicious and hearty addition to your meals or as a tasty snack on their own! Adjust the seasoning and spices according to your taste preferences to customize the flavor of your sausages.

Perník (Czech Gingerbread)

Ingredients:

- 3 cups all-purpose flour
- 1 teaspoon baking soda
- 2 teaspoons ground cinnamon
- 1 teaspoon ground ginger
- 1/2 teaspoon ground cloves
- 1/2 teaspoon ground nutmeg
- 1/4 teaspoon ground allspice
- 1/4 teaspoon salt
- 1 cup unsalted butter, softened
- 1 cup granulated sugar
- 2 large eggs
- 1/2 cup honey
- 1/2 cup sour cream
- Zest of 1 lemon
- Zest of 1 orange

For the glaze (optional):

- 1 cup powdered sugar
- 1-2 tablespoons milk

Instructions:

Preheat your oven to 350°F (175°C). Grease and flour a 9x13-inch baking pan or line it with parchment paper.
In a medium bowl, whisk together the flour, baking soda, ground cinnamon, ground ginger, ground cloves, ground nutmeg, ground allspice, and salt. Set aside.
In a large mixing bowl, cream together the softened butter and granulated sugar until light and fluffy.
Beat in the eggs, one at a time, until well combined. Add the honey, sour cream, lemon zest, and orange zest, and mix until smooth.
Gradually add the dry ingredients to the wet ingredients, mixing until a smooth batter forms.

Pour the batter into the prepared baking pan, spreading it out evenly.

Bake in the preheated oven for 25-30 minutes, or until a toothpick inserted into the center comes out clean.

Remove the gingerbread from the oven and let it cool in the pan for about 10 minutes before transferring it to a wire rack to cool completely.

If desired, prepare the glaze by whisking together the powdered sugar and milk until smooth. Drizzle the glaze over the cooled gingerbread.

Once the glaze has set, slice the perník into squares or rectangles and serve. Enjoy this delicious Czech Gingerbread as a festive treat with a cup of tea or coffee!

You can also customize your perník by adding chopped nuts, dried fruits, or chocolate chips to the batter for added texture and flavor. Store any leftover gingerbread in an airtight container at room temperature for several days.

Pstruh na Paprice (Trout with Paprika Sauce)

Ingredients:

- 4 trout fillets, skin-on
- Salt and pepper to taste
- 2 tablespoons all-purpose flour
- 2 tablespoons vegetable oil
- 1 onion, finely chopped
- 2 cloves garlic, minced
- 2 tablespoons sweet paprika
- 1 cup chicken or vegetable broth
- 1/2 cup sour cream
- Chopped fresh parsley for garnish
- Lemon wedges for serving

Instructions:

Season the trout fillets with salt and pepper on both sides. Dust them lightly with flour, shaking off any excess.

In a large skillet, heat the vegetable oil over medium-high heat. Add the trout fillets, skin-side down, and cook for 3-4 minutes until the skin is golden and crispy. Carefully flip the fillets and cook for another 2-3 minutes until cooked through. Remove the trout from the skillet and set aside.

In the same skillet, add the chopped onion and garlic. Sauté until softened and fragrant, about 2-3 minutes.

Stir in the sweet paprika and cook for another minute, allowing the flavors to meld together.

Pour in the chicken or vegetable broth, stirring to combine. Bring the mixture to a simmer and let it cook for 3-4 minutes to reduce slightly.

Reduce the heat to low and stir in the sour cream until well combined. Simmer the sauce gently for another 2-3 minutes, stirring occasionally, until heated through.

Return the cooked trout fillets to the skillet, spooning the paprika sauce over them. Cook for another 1-2 minutes, just until the fish is heated through.

Sprinkle the trout with chopped fresh parsley for garnish.

Serve the pstruh na paprice hot, accompanied by lemon wedges for squeezing over the fish.

Enjoy this flavorful Czech Trout with Paprika Sauce as a delicious and satisfying main course!

Serve the trout with sides such as boiled potatoes, rice, or steamed vegetables to complete the meal. The creamy paprika sauce adds a wonderful depth of flavor to the tender and flaky fish, making it a favorite among Czech cuisine enthusiasts.

Třešňový Závin (Cherry Strudel)

Ingredients:

For the dough:

- 2 cups all-purpose flour
- 1/4 teaspoon salt
- 1/4 cup vegetable oil
- 3/4 cup lukewarm water
- 1 tablespoon white vinegar

For the cherry filling:

- 4 cups pitted cherries (fresh or frozen)
- 1/2 cup granulated sugar
- 1 tablespoon cornstarch
- 1 tablespoon lemon juice
- 1 teaspoon vanilla extract
- Zest of 1 lemon (optional)

For assembling:

- 2 tablespoons unsalted butter, melted
- Powdered sugar for dusting (optional)

Instructions:

Preheat your oven to 375°F (190°C). Line a baking sheet with parchment paper. In a large mixing bowl, combine the flour and salt. Make a well in the center and add the vegetable oil, lukewarm water, and white vinegar. Mix until a smooth dough forms. If the dough is too sticky, add a little more flour.
Knead the dough on a floured surface for about 5-7 minutes, or until it becomes smooth and elastic. Form the dough into a ball, cover it with a clean kitchen towel, and let it rest for about 30 minutes.

While the dough is resting, prepare the cherry filling. In a mixing bowl, combine the pitted cherries, granulated sugar, cornstarch, lemon juice, vanilla extract, and lemon zest (if using). Toss until the cherries are evenly coated.

Roll out the dough on a floured surface into a large rectangle, about 1/8 inch thick.

Brush the melted butter over the rolled-out dough, leaving a border around the edges.

Spread the cherry filling evenly over the buttered dough.

Starting from one long side, carefully roll up the dough jelly-roll style, enclosing the filling.

Transfer the rolled strudel onto the prepared baking sheet, seam side down.

Brush the top of the strudel with a little extra melted butter for a golden finish.

Bake the strudel in the preheated oven for about 30-35 minutes, or until it is golden brown and crispy.

Remove the strudel from the oven and let it cool slightly on the baking sheet.

Once cooled, dust the cherry strudel with powdered sugar, if desired.

Slice the strudel into pieces and serve warm or at room temperature.

Enjoy the delicious Czech třešňový závin (Cherry Strudel) as a delightful dessert or sweet treat!

Feel free to customize the filling by using other fruits like apples or peaches, or adding chopped nuts or cinnamon for extra flavor.

Kávový Koláč (Coffee Cake)

Ingredients:

For the cake:

- 2 cups all-purpose flour
- 1 cup granulated sugar
- 1/2 cup unsalted butter, softened
- 1/2 cup sour cream
- 2 eggs
- 1 teaspoon vanilla extract
- 1 teaspoon baking powder
- 1/2 teaspoon baking soda
- 1/4 teaspoon salt

For the coffee topping:

- 1/2 cup brewed strong coffee, cooled
- 2 tablespoons granulated sugar
- 1 teaspoon instant coffee granules
- 1/2 teaspoon ground cinnamon

For the glaze (optional):

- 1/2 cup powdered sugar
- 1-2 tablespoons milk
- 1/2 teaspoon vanilla extract

Instructions:

Preheat your oven to 350°F (175°C). Grease and flour a 9x13-inch baking dish or line it with parchment paper.
In a large mixing bowl, cream together the softened butter and granulated sugar until light and fluffy.
Beat in the eggs, one at a time, until well combined. Stir in the sour cream and vanilla extract.

In a separate bowl, whisk together the flour, baking powder, baking soda, and salt. Gradually add the dry ingredients to the wet ingredients, mixing until a smooth batter forms.

Spread the batter evenly into the prepared baking dish.

In a small bowl, stir together the brewed strong coffee, granulated sugar, instant coffee granules, and ground cinnamon until the sugar is dissolved.

Pour the coffee mixture evenly over the cake batter.

Bake in the preheated oven for 25-30 minutes, or until a toothpick inserted into the center comes out clean.

Remove the cake from the oven and let it cool in the baking dish for about 10 minutes.

If desired, prepare the glaze by whisking together the powdered sugar, milk, and vanilla extract until smooth. Drizzle the glaze over the cooled cake.

Slice the kávový koláč into squares and serve.

Enjoy this delicious Czech Coffee Cake as a delightful dessert or sweet treat with your favorite hot beverage!

Feel free to customize this coffee cake by adding chopped nuts, chocolate chips, or a streusel topping before baking for extra flavor and texture.

Bílá Klobása (White Sausage)

Ingredients:

- 1 kg ground pork (you can also use a mixture of pork and veal or beef)
- 1 onion, finely chopped
- 2 cloves garlic, minced
- 2 teaspoons salt
- 1 teaspoon ground white pepper
- 1/2 teaspoon ground nutmeg
- 1/2 teaspoon ground allspice
- 1/4 teaspoon ground ginger
- 1/4 teaspoon ground marjoram
- 1/4 teaspoon ground caraway seeds
- 1/4 cup breadcrumbs
- 1/4 cup milk
- Hog casings (natural sausage casings)

Instructions:

Rinse the hog casings under cold water to remove any salt and debris. Soak them in lukewarm water for at least 30 minutes to soften.

In a large mixing bowl, combine the ground pork with the chopped onion, minced garlic, salt, white pepper, nutmeg, allspice, ginger, marjoram, caraway seeds, breadcrumbs, and milk. Mix well until all the ingredients are evenly distributed throughout the meat.

Prepare your sausage stuffer according to the manufacturer's instructions, and thread the softened hog casings onto the nozzle.

Stuff the seasoned meat mixture into the hog casings, ensuring that the sausages are evenly filled but not overstuffed to avoid bursting during cooking. Twist the sausages into links of your desired length.

Once all the sausages are stuffed, you can either poach or boil them:

- Poaching: Bring a pot of water to a gentle simmer (around 170°F or 77°C). Submerge the sausages in the water and poach them for about 20-30 minutes, or until they reach an internal temperature of 160°F (71°C).
- Boiling: Bring a pot of water to a boil. Reduce the heat to low and add the sausages. Simmer them gently for about 20-30 minutes, or until they are cooked through.

Once cooked, remove the sausages from the water and let them cool slightly before serving.

Serve the bílá klobása hot with your favorite condiments, such as mustard or horseradish.

Enjoy these homemade Czech white sausages as a delicious and hearty addition to your meals!

Feel free to adjust the seasonings and spices according to your taste preferences. You can also experiment with adding other herbs and flavors to customize the sausages to your liking.

Kynuté Knedlíky (Yeast Dumplings)

Ingredients:

- 500g (about 4 cups) all-purpose flour
- 1 packet (7g) active dry yeast
- 1 cup lukewarm milk
- 2 tablespoons granulated sugar
- 1 teaspoon salt
- 2 eggs
- 2 tablespoons unsalted butter, melted

Instructions:

In a small bowl, combine the lukewarm milk and granulated sugar. Sprinkle the active dry yeast over the milk mixture and let it sit for about 5-10 minutes, or until foamy.
In a large mixing bowl, sift the flour and salt together. Make a well in the center.
In a separate bowl, beat the eggs lightly.
Pour the yeast mixture and beaten eggs into the well of the flour.
Using a wooden spoon or your hands, gradually incorporate the flour into the wet ingredients until a dough forms.
Knead the dough on a floured surface for about 5-10 minutes, or until it becomes smooth and elastic.
Shape the dough into a ball and place it in a lightly greased bowl. Cover the bowl with a clean kitchen towel or plastic wrap and let the dough rise in a warm, draft-free place for about 1-1.5 hours, or until it doubles in size.
Once the dough has risen, punch it down to release the air.
Divide the dough into portions and shape them into round dumplings, about the size of a tennis ball.
Place the dumplings on a floured surface, cover them with a clean kitchen towel, and let them rise again for about 30 minutes.
Bring a large pot of salted water to a boil.
Gently drop the risen dumplings into the boiling water. Reduce the heat to low and simmer the dumplings for about 15-20 minutes, turning them occasionally, until they are cooked through and puffed up.
Use a slotted spoon to remove the cooked dumplings from the water and drain them on a clean kitchen towel.

Serve the kynuté knedlíky hot as a side dish with your favorite meat and gravy, or let them cool slightly and serve them filled with fruit and topped with melted butter and powdered sugar for a sweet dessert.

Enjoy these fluffy and delicious Czech Yeast Dumplings as a versatile addition to your meals!

Bramboráčky (Potato Patties)

Ingredients:

- 4 large potatoes, peeled and grated
- 1 small onion, grated
- 2 eggs
- 1/4 cup all-purpose flour
- 1 teaspoon salt
- 1/2 teaspoon ground black pepper
- Vegetable oil for frying
- Sour cream and chopped fresh parsley for serving (optional)

Instructions:

Place the grated potatoes in a clean kitchen towel and squeeze out as much excess moisture as possible.
In a large mixing bowl, combine the grated potatoes, grated onion, eggs, flour, salt, and pepper. Mix well until all the ingredients are evenly combined.
Heat a thin layer of vegetable oil in a large skillet over medium heat.
Take a small handful of the potato mixture and shape it into a patty, about 1/4 to 1/2 inch thick. Repeat with the remaining mixture, placing the patties in the hot oil.
Fry the potato patties for 3-4 minutes on each side, or until golden brown and crispy. You may need to fry them in batches depending on the size of your skillet.
Once cooked, transfer the potato patties to a paper towel-lined plate to drain any excess oil.
Serve the bramboráčky hot, garnished with sour cream and chopped fresh parsley if desired.
Enjoy these delicious Czech Potato Patties as a savory side dish or a tasty snack!

Feel free to customize the potato patties by adding grated cheese, chopped herbs, or spices to the mixture for extra flavor. You can also serve them with ketchup or a dipping sauce of your choice.

Lívance (Czech Pancakes)

Ingredients:

- 2 cups all-purpose flour
- 1 tablespoon granulated sugar
- 1/2 teaspoon salt
- 1 packet (7g) active dry yeast
- 1 cup lukewarm milk
- 2 large eggs
- 2 tablespoons unsalted butter, melted
- Vegetable oil for frying
- Powdered sugar for dusting (optional)
- Fruit, jam, or whipped cream for topping (optional)

Instructions:

In a small bowl, dissolve the granulated sugar and active dry yeast in lukewarm milk. Let it sit for about 5-10 minutes, or until foamy.

In a large mixing bowl, whisk together the flour and salt.

Make a well in the center of the flour mixture and pour in the yeast mixture, melted butter, and eggs.

Using a whisk or electric mixer, beat the ingredients together until a smooth batter forms. The batter will be thick and somewhat lumpy.

Cover the bowl with a clean kitchen towel or plastic wrap and let the batter rise in a warm, draft-free place for about 30-45 minutes, or until it doubles in size and becomes bubbly.

Heat a non-stick skillet or griddle over medium heat and lightly grease it with vegetable oil.

Using a spoon or a small ladle, drop dollops of the batter onto the hot skillet, forming small pancakes, about 2-3 inches in diameter.

Cook the livance for about 2-3 minutes on each side, or until they are golden brown and cooked through.

Transfer the cooked livance to a plate lined with paper towels to absorb any excess oil.

Repeat the process with the remaining batter, adding more oil to the skillet as needed.

Serve the livance hot, sprinkled with powdered sugar and topped with your favorite fruit, jam, or whipped cream if desired.

Enjoy these delicious Czech pancakes as a sweet breakfast, snack, or dessert!

Feel free to customize the livance by adding grated lemon zest, cinnamon, or vanilla extract to the batter for extra flavor. You can also serve them with maple syrup or honey for a sweeter taste.

www.ingramcontent.com/pod-product-compliance
Lightning Source LLC
LaVergne TN
LVHW081616060526
838201LV00054B/2276